300    400 Feet

BOAT DECK
A
B
C
D
E
F
LOWER

1ST CL. PROMENADE          FIRST CLASS
READING & WRITING ROOM          1ST CLASS
BOILER UPTAKE CASING          VENT TRUNK          BOILER UPTAKE CASING
CORRIDOR          ENTRANCE

ENS WITH LARGE WINDOWS
PORT & STARBD

FIRST CLASS          FORECASTLE DECK.
SITTING ROOM          1ST CLASS
BOILER UPTAKE CASING          BOILER UPTAKE CASING          STEAM WINCHES          CAPSTAN          CAPSTAN
ENTRANCE          STEAM WINCH          NO.1 HOLD          CAPSTAN          CAPSTAN
SUITE OF ROOMS          PARLOUR SUITE
SITTING ROOM

# EXPLORE TITANIC

### BREATHTAKING NEW PICTURES, RECREATED WITH DIGITAL TECHNOLOGY

Peter Chrisp

With illustrations by
Somchith Vongprachanh

BARRON'S

## THIS IS A CARLTON BOOK

Original concept: *Darren Jordan*
Project Editor: *Paul Virr*
Written by: *Peter Chrisp*
Creative Director: *Darren Jordan*
Illustrator: *Somchith Vongprachanh*
Designer: *Danny Baldwin*
Picture Research: *Steve Behan*
Additional photography: *Karl Adamson*
Production: *Kate Pimm*

First edition for North America published in 2011 by Barron's Educational Series, Inc.

Text and artwork copyright: © 2011 Carlton Books Ltd.
Design copyright: © 2011 Carlton Books Ltd.

*All inquiries should be addressed to:*
Barron's Educational Series, Inc,
250 Wireless Boulevard
Hauppauge, NY 11788
**www.barronseduc.com**

ISBN: 978-1-4380-7159-6

Library of Congress Control Number: 2011920288

Printed in China.
Printed by RR Donnelley-South China, Dongguann, China.
Date of Manufacture: December 2011
10 9 8 7 6 5 4 3 2

## PICTURE CREDITS

The publishers would like to thank the following sources for their kind permission to reproduce the pictures in this book.

### THE BIG IDEA 4-5
Mary Evans Picture Library (*Mauretania*), Getty Images/ SSPL (Lord William Pirrie), © Reproduced courtesy of National Museums Northern Ireland (James Bruce Ismay), © Reproduced courtesy of National Museums Northern Ireland (*Olympic* & *Titanic* advertisement), Corbis/Sean Sexton Collection (planning office), Corbis/The Mariners' Museum (section of *Titanic*), Corbis/Underwood & Underwood (Thomas Andrews)

### BUILDING TITANIC 6-7
Topfoto.co.uk (*Titanic* construction), © National Museums Northern Ireland 2011 Collection Harland & Wolff, Ulster Folk & Transport Museum (Harland & Wolff Advertisement), (H 1919) © National Museums Northern Ireland 2011, Collection Harland & Wolff, Ulster Folk & Transport Museum (Hydraulic riveting, at bottom of sheer stroke, *Britannic*, 25 May 1913), Science Photo Library (propeller), Corbis/Michael Maloney/San Francisco Chronicle (*Titanic* artifact)

### READY TO SAIL 8-9
(TR59-4) © National Museums Northern Ireland 2011 Collection Ulster Folk & Transport Museum (*Titanic* launch invitation), Mary Evans Picture Library (*Titanic* boiler lifted), Corbis/Hulton-Deutsch Collection (trial run), Corbis/Ralph White (Captain E.J. Smith), © National Museums Northern Ireland 2011 Collection Ulster Folk & Transport Museum (*Titanic* at wharf, Southampton, 10 April 1912, Courtney #5), Carlton Books (whistle)

### THE VOYAGE BEGINS 10-11
Getty Images (mailbags carried on board), reproduced courtesy of National Museums Northern Ireland 2011 (postcard from the *Titanic*), Father Browne S.J. Collection (Irish passengers), Mary Evans Picture Library (map), Getty Images (binoculars, Francis Browne & stern view of *Titanic*)

### FULL STEAM AHEAD 12-13
(H 1711) Reproduced courtesy of National Museums Northern Ireland (engine), Alamy (steam room), Corbis/ Bettmann (Straus)

### WELCOME ABOARD 14-15
Southampton City Council (steward), Father Browne S.J. Collection (passenger)

### TRAVELING FIRST CLASS 16-17
Reproduced courtesy of National Museums Northern Ireland (first-class bathroom (H401-C), Rex Features/ Richard Gardner (cabin)

### OUT AND ABOUT 18-19
Rex Features/John Lodge (deck chair), Rex Features/Sipa Press (Café Parisien and cup and saucer), Getty Images (gym), Mary Evans Picture Library/Onslow Auctions Limited (Turkish bath)

### A DIP IN THE POOL 20-21
Carlton Books (F deck swimming pool & changing rooms), Mary Evans Picture Library (publicity photo of *Titanic* pool), © Copyright 2005 Ohrstrom Library, and St. Paul's School (Colonel Archibald Gracie)

### DINNER IS SERVED 22-23
Topfoto.co.uk/PA (menu), Rex Features/Sipa Press (china plate), Getty Images (Lady Duff Gordon)

### SECOND CLASS 24-25
Topfoto.co.uk (Second Class Passengers & Laurence Beesley), Mary Evans Picture Library (cabin)

### IN STEERAGE 26-27
Rex Features/Phil Yeomans (notebook), Father Browne S. J. Collection (passengers), Reproduced courtesy of National Museums Northern Ireland (third-class reading room and third-class state room), Private Collection (third-class dining room), Rex Features/Peter Brooker (cup and saucer)

### DISASTER STRIKES 28-29
Rex Features/Nils Jorgensen (ship's bell), Topfoto.co.uk/ PA (First Officer William Murdoch)

### ABANDON SHIP! 30-31
Mary Evans Picture Library (iceberg), Rex Features/ Stanley Lehrer Collection (life jacket), Corbis/Hulton-Deutsch Collection (lifeboats), Getty Images (radio operator), Topfoto.co.uk (Jack Phillips)

### GATEFOLD
Getty Images (flare)

### TO THE LIFEBOATS 32-33
Corbis/Bettmann (lifeboats lowered, illustration, Molly Brown), Mary Evans Picture Library/Illustrated London News (Charles Lightoller), Topfoto.co.uk (Charles Hendrickson, postcard, Countess Rothes)

### LAST MOMENTS 34-35
Corbis/Bettmann (Benjamin Guggenheim), Mary Evans Picture Library/Illustrated London News (musicians)

### THE RESCUE 36-37
Mary Evans Picture Library/Illustrated London News (*Carpathia*, survivors aboard *Carpathia* & rescued survivors), Getty Images (Rostron) Mary Evans Picture Library/Onslow Auctions Limited (medal), Corbis/ Bettmann (lifeboat)

### AFTER THE TRAGEDY 38-39
Corbis/Bettmann (Ismay), Getty Images (newspaper boy), Alamy/Colin Palmer Photography (memorial), Istockphoto.com (record player), Rex Features/Everett Collection (film posters)

### TITANIC TODAY 40-41
Corbis/Ralph White (bow of *Titanic*, dishes, propeller), Rex Features/Tony Kyriacou (hat)

All other images are 3D-rendered, created by Somchith Vongprachanh, © Carlton Books Ltd.

Every effort has been made to acknowledge correctly and contact the source and/or copyright holder of each picture, and Carlton Books Limited apologizes for any unintentional errors or omissions, which will be corrected in future editions of this book.

# EXPLORE TITANIC

No other ship has captured the imagination as powerfully as *Titanic*, yet just a handful of black-and-white photographs remain to give us an idea of how the ship really looked—until now.

We have gone back to the original plans to digitally recreate *Titanic* using ultra-real 3D graphics. Finally, you can see *Titanic* as she was, in color and in all her glory. These amazing new views of *Titanic* are so real that you won't believe your eyes!

Swimming Pool

Grand Central Staircase

Second-class Promenade

Wheelhouse

First-class Dining Saloon

# THE BIG IDEA

The early 1900s were the golden age of the ocean liner, with more than a million people emigrating from Europe to the U.S. each year. Two British shipping companies competed for passengers who wished to cross the Atlantic: White Star and Cunard.

R.M.S. "MAURETANIA."

### RIVALS FOR THE RIBAND

The liner that made the fastest Atlantic crossing was allowed to fly a long blue banner known as the Blue Riband from the mast. In 1907, Cunard beat White Star to the prize with the *Mauretania* and kept it for 22 years.

At its launch, RMS *Mauretania* was the fastest ship in the world. With a top speed of about 26 knots, it could cross the Atlantic in a week.

### BIGGER AND BETTER

Cunard's success worried James Bruce Ismay, the Managing Director of White Star, and his ship-building partner, Lord William Pirrie. In 1907, they came up with a plan to give them the edge over Cunard. White Star would build three huge liners, the world's largest passenger ships, each one-and-a-half times larger than Cunard's *Mauretania*.

LORD WILLIAM PIRRIE

JAMES BRUCE ISMAY

## SAILING IN STYLE

White Star's new liners wouldn't be as fast as the *Mauretania*, but they would earn more money by carrying more passengers. They would also attract the richest customers by being incredibly luxurious. The design and the furniture would be so grand that passengers might think they were in a posh hotel rather than on board a ship.

It took several months to design *Titanic*, here in the Harland and Wolff drawing office.

In their advertising, White Star boasted about the sheer size of the first two new ships, *Olympic* and *Titanic*.

## MAKING PLANS

The new ships would be built in Belfast by Lord Pirrie's company, Harland and Wolff. Thomas Andrews, Pirrie's nephew, was head of its design department. Andrews and his team now set about designing the largest ships ever to be built. They made thousands of detailed plans, all drawn by hand. Andrews was very proud of their work and thought that *Titanic* was the perfect ship.

Watertight compartments

## UNSINKABLE?

For safety, the designers divided the lower part of each ship into 16 watertight compartments. In an emergency, these compartments would be sealed off by electrically operated doors. The ship could then stay afloat—as long as no more than two compartments were flooded.

*"This ship is as nearly perfect as human brains can make her."*

**Thomas Andrews to a passenger on *Titanic***

THOMAS ANDREWS

# BUILDING TITANIC

With the plans complete, the massive task of building *Titanic* and her sister ships, *Olympic* and *Britannic*, began. It took the Harland and Wolff shipyards two years to build them.

*Titanic* was built on the slipway she would be launched from. The gantry surrounding the ship was 228 ft (69 m) high.

### BUILT IN BELFAST

Harland and Wolff was the world's leading shipbuilding company. Based in Belfast, Ireland, it used the latest technology and was known for getting work done on time and on budget.

# HARLAND & WOLFF, LIMITED.

Builders of the "OLYMPIC" and "TITANIC," the largest steamers in the World, 45,000 tons each.

BELFAST WORKS.

This advertisement for Harland and Wolff shows the huge scale of the shipyards where *Titanic* was built.

### A TITANIC TEAM

It took a workforce of about 3,000 men and boys to build *Titanic*. It was dangerous work—more than 450 of them were injured and 17 died during construction.

### FIRST STEPS

Before work could begin, two new slipways were built between a massive steel framework called a gantry. The gantry was used for moveable cranes.

### WORK BEGINS

The first part of the ship to be built was the keel—the metal backbone of the ship. The keel was laid down on March 31, 1909 and stretched for 883 ft (269 m)—longer than two soccer fields.

### SHIP SHAPE

Along the keel, a series of curved metal ribs called frames were added. These gave *Titanic* its shape. The metal plates that made up the outer shell of the ship would later be attached to the frames.

A riveter using a hydraulic riveting machine. It took five years of on-the-job training to become a skilled riveter.

## WATERTIGHT

The next job was to attach sheets of steel to the outside of the ship to make a watertight hull. The outer skin of *Titanic* was made of steel plates, 1 in. (2.5 cm) thick. These hull plates were held in place with iron or steel rivets.

## FIXING THE PLATES

At the bow and stern of *Titanic*, all the rivets were fixed by hand by a manual riveting team of three men and two boys. In the central section of the ship, where there was more room, bulky new riveting machines could be used.

More than 3 million rivets were used. The workers were paid for each rivet fitted, so they worked as quickly as they could!

At the stern, the workers fitted the central propeller and two side propellers that would drive the ship along.

## RIVETING

Riveting was a highly skilled job. Each rivet was heated in a furnace until it was red hot, then it was placed in a hole on the hull plate and the ends were hammered flat.

# READY TO SAIL

Soon after noon, on May 31, 1911, *Titanic* was launched. A crowd of 100,000 cheered as the ship took just over a minute to slide down the slipway into the water.

### LAUNCH DAY

At its launch, *Titanic* was mostly an empty shell, yet she still weighed around 26,000 tons—making her the heaviest object ever moved by people. She was pushed down the greased slipway with a machine operated by the shipyard manager, Charles Payne.

Launch
OF
White Star Royal Mail Triple-Screw Steamer

## "TITANIC"

At BELFAST,

Wednesday, 31st May, 1911, at 12-15 p.m.

Admit Bearer.

The White Star Line sold tickets to watch the launch of *Titanic*. All the money raised went to charity.

One of *Titanic*'s huge boilers being lifted into the empty shell of the ship, which had yet to be fitted with its four funnels.

### FIXTURES AND FITTINGS

After the launch, *Titanic* was towed to the deepwater outfitting wharf, where work continued on her for more than ten months. Here the engines, funnels, and the luxurious interiors were fitted.

### TEST DRIVE

Before she could carry passengers, *Titanic* had to pass a series of tests called sea trials. On April 2, 1912, she was towed to the open waters of Belfast Lough where she sailed under her own power for the first time.

### SEAWORTHY

The ship made circles at various speeds. In an emergency-stop test it took her three minutes and 15 seconds to come to a halt and she covered 2,549 ft (777 m). This was satisfactory for such a large vessel, and *Titanic* was officially declared seaworthy.

Pulled by five tugs, *Titanic* enters Belfast Lough for her sea trials.

## SAILING TO SOUTHAMPTON

Immediately after passing her sea trials, *Titanic* set sail for Southampton, with a small crew under the command of Captain E. J. Smith. He was the most experienced captain of the White Star Line, and had previously been captain of *Titanic*'s sister ship, *Olympic*.

*"In forty years at sea...I never saw a wreck and never have been wrecked."* **Captain E. J. Smith**

CAPTAIN
E. J. SMITH

## FINISHING TOUCHES

At midnight on April 3, 1912, *Titanic* reached Southampton. Over the next week, 724 more crew members joined the ship and vast quantities of stores were loaded. The final touches were also made to the ship's interior decoration, as carpets were laid and curtains hung.

## TAKING ON PASSENGERS

On the morning of Wednesday, April 10, about 1,000 passengers came aboard and were shown to their cabins. Finally, at noon, *Titanic* set off on her first voyage, bound for France, Ireland, and America.

Before departure, the ship's whistles sounded three blasts that could be heard across the city.

*Titanic*, moored in Southampton, where a massive new dock had been built for the huge White Star liners.

# THE VOYAGE BEGINS

*Titanic* made two short stops to take aboard more passengers, at Cherbourg in France and Queenstown in Ireland. On April 11, she finally set sail for New York, carrying 1,324 passengers and 899 crew.

## A FLOATING POST OFFICE

At each stop, the ship also picked up sacks of mail—more than 4,500 sacks holding some 400,000 letters. These, plus all the mail sent by the passengers, would be sorted during the voyage by the ship's five postal clerks.

These mailbags, carried aboard in Queenstown, were filled with letters from Irish people to relatives who had emigrated to the U.S.

WHITE STAR LINE

Triple-Screw R.M.S. "OLYMPIC" and "TITANIC." 45,000 Tons each. The Largest Steamers in the World.

## ROYAL MAIL SHIP

The ship's full title was RMS *Titanic*, the initials RMS standing for Royal Mail Ship. Royal Mail Ships had to be fast and reliable. A ship that delivered the mail late would be fined and could lose its official RMS title.

In Queenstown, a passenger named Robert Phillips sent this postcard to a friend, saying, "We are all right up to now and having a jolly time."

## FAREWELL TO IRELAND

On the Queenstown harbor front, 123 Irish passengers said tearful farewells to relatives and joined the ship. All but ten had third-class tickets. They were mostly poor young men and women from the countryside, hoping to find a better life in America.

WHITESTARLINE | AMERICANLINE.

Irish passengers wait on the White Star wharf in Queenstown (now Cobh) in Ireland, photographed from *Titanic* by Francis Browne before he left the ship.

> "*So far we are having a delightful trip. The weather is beautiful and the ship magnificent...it's like a floating town.*"
>
> **Passenger Harvey Collyer in a letter to his parents, April 11, 1912**

At sea, the lookouts discovered that their binoculars had been lost, so they would have to rely on the naked eye alone.

FRANCIS BROWNE

### ONE LAST PICTURE

Francis Browne, a student priest and a keen amateur photographer, left *Titanic* in Queenstown with his camera and dozens of photographic plates. His pictures are the only visual record of the ship's voyage.

Francis Browne took one of the last pictures of *Titanic*, as she left Ireland, her stern crowded with third-class passengers.

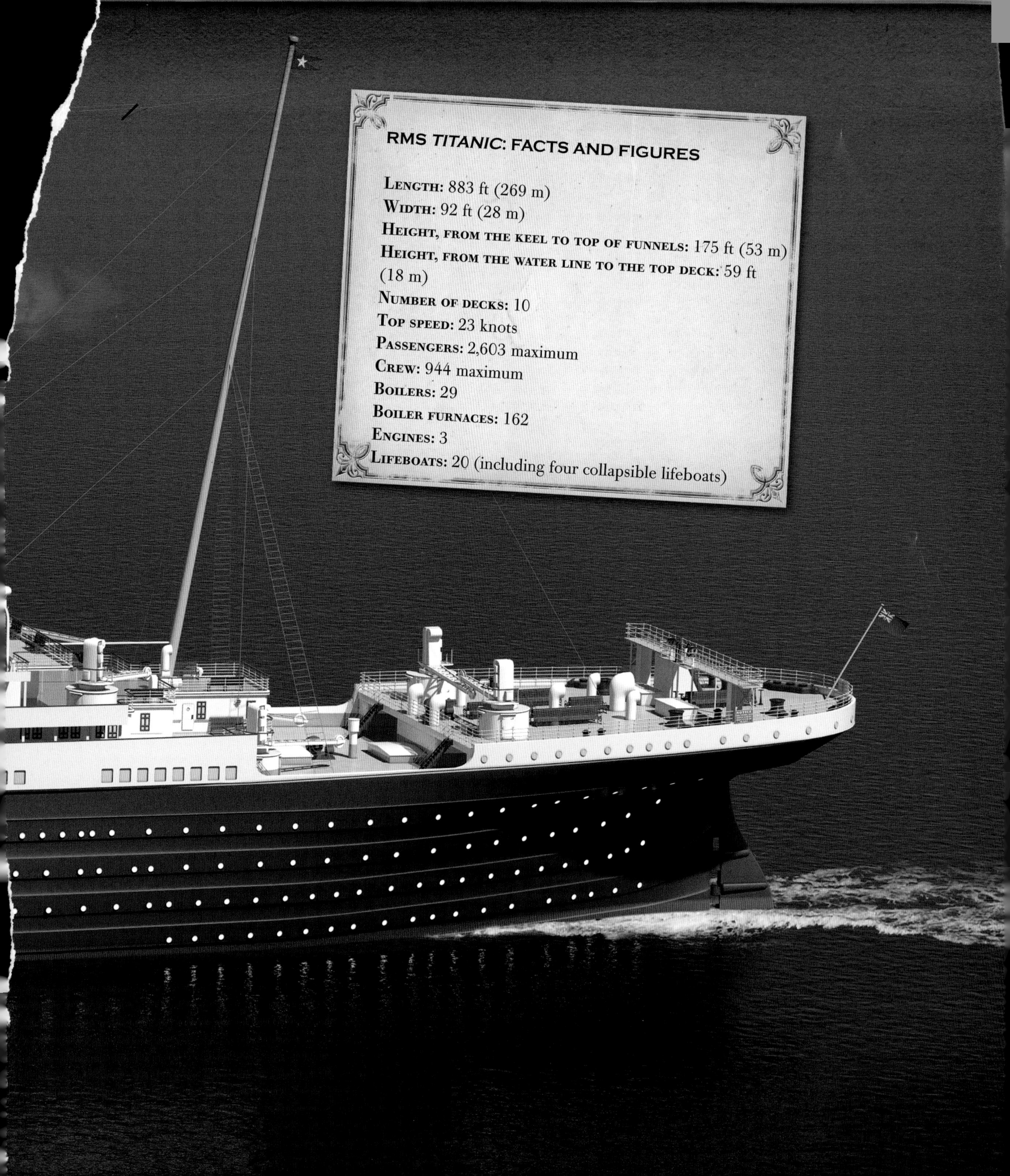

## RMS *TITANIC*: FACTS AND FIGURES

**LENGTH:** 883 ft (269 m)

**WIDTH:** 92 ft (28 m)

**HEIGHT, FROM THE KEEL TO TOP OF FUNNELS:** 175 ft (53 m)

**HEIGHT, FROM THE WATER LINE TO THE TOP DECK:** 59 ft (18 m)

**NUMBER OF DECKS:** 10

**TOP SPEED:** 23 knots

**PASSENGERS:** 2,603 maximum

**CREW:** 944 maximum

**BOILERS:** 29

**BOILER FURNACES:** 162

**ENGINES:** 3

**LIFEBOATS:** 20 (including four collapsible lifeboats)

**RMS *Titanic* Under Way in the Atlantic Ocean**
*As* Titanic *sails past, you can see two flags fluttering from the masts.*
*The U.S. Stars and Stripes, on the forward mast, showed her destination.*
*On the rear mast, she flew the emblem of the White Star Line.*

# FULL STEAM AHEAD

Everything on *Titanic* was driven by steam power, from the ship's propellers to the lights, heating, and the elevators. Steam was provided by 29 massive boilers, heated by 162 coal-burning furnaces.

## STEAM POWER

The boilers produced steam, which was fed to three massive engines, each turning one of the ship's propellers. In the rear of the ship, the steam powered four smaller engines to generate electricity for the whole ship.

The engines that drove the propellers were as tall as a three-story house.

## FEEDING THE FURNACES

Below decks, teams of stokers shoveled coal into the furnaces that heated the boilers. They also raked out about 100 tons of ash a day. The work was hot and dangerous. Stokers wore clogs to protect their feet from burning coals.

## DIRTY WORK

In the bunkers above and between the boilers, "trimmers" kept the coal level and shoveled it down chutes to the stokers below. It was a filthy job, and they wore wet rags over their faces to keep out the coal dust.

*Titanic's* 176 stokers and 73 trimmers were usually covered in black coal dust, so they were nicknamed the "black gang."

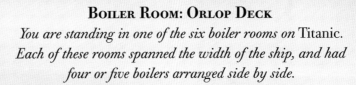

### BOILER ROOM: ORLOP DECK
*You are standing in one of the six boiler rooms on* Titanic.
*Each of these rooms spanned the width of the ship, and had*
*four or five boilers arranged side by side.*

# WELCOME ABOARD

*Titanic* was designed to be the most luxurious ship in the world, with lavish interiors to rival the grand hotels. As a first-class passenger, you would travel in style, right from the moment you caught the special first-class boat train to Southampton.

## A FIRST-CLASS WELCOME

The ship carried 325 first-class passengers, including several U.S. millionaires. Many traveled with servants, maids, nurses, and chauffeurs. Their staterooms, some with their own private decks, were on the ship's upper levels, far from the noise of the engines. As they walked down the Grand Central Staircase, they would have felt as if they had just arrived for a stay in an expensive hotel.

First-class passengers walk up the gangplank to the Boat Deck as they board *Titanic* in Southampton.

## STEWARDS AND STEWARDESSES

Passengers were looked after by an army of stewards and stewardesses, each wearing a numbered badge. They took care of all the daily needs of passengers: helping them dress, cleaning their rooms, bringing drinks, walking their dogs, and even comforting them if they felt seasick.

Stewards wore neat white jackets that made them easy to recognize. They could be called at any time with an electric bell

**A Deck: Grand Central Staircase**

*You are standing before the Grand Central Staircase in first class.*
*This impressive sweep of stairs greeted first-class passengers as they*
*came down from the Boat Deck into the luxurious interior of the ship.*

# TRAVELING FIRST CLASS

*Titanic* had 39 first-class suites on decks B and C, decorated in the styles of different historical periods. The suites included bedrooms, bathrooms, toilets, elegant lounges, and extra rooms for servants.

## UPPER CLASS

The suites and individual first-class cabins were all on the upper levels, far from the noise of the engines and within easy reach of the Promenade Deck. They were central, too, so first-class passengers didn't have far to walk to the Grand Central Staircase or the elevators.

This recreation of a first-class cabin from a museum shows how luxurious *Titanic*'s cabins would have looked.

## EVERY CONVENIENCE

An added luxury for the wealthiest passengers was a first-class cabin with its own private bathroom. These had hot and cold water, plus a modern shower spray. Other passengers had to use the public baths.

This White Star publicity picture shows one of the first-class bathrooms.

### JOHN JACOB ASTOR

The richest passenger was John Jacob Astor, a millionaire who was returning to the U.S. with his new wife. They traveled with a valet, a maid, a nurse, and a pet dog called Kitty, and occupied first-class cabins C62-4.

*"What a ship! Our rooms are furnished in the best of taste and most luxuriously...they are really rooms, not cabins."*

**Ida Straus, letter to a friend, posted from *Titanic* in Southampton**

ISIDOR STRAUS

IDA STRAUS

## THE STRAUS SUITE

One of the most luxurious of the first-class suites was number C55-7, occupied by Isidor and Ida Straus. Their suite included rooms for their maid, Ellen Bird, and a manservant, John Farthing.

Titanic's desk lamps were specially designed to stay level, even when the ship tilted.

# OUT AND ABOUT

First-class passengers found plenty to do onboard. They could walk on the Promenade Deck or use the gymnasium, squash court, and swimming pool. To relax, they could visit the Turkish bath or one of the cafés.

"*I had a long promenade and a doze for an hour up to five o'clock. The band played in the afternoon for tea, but I savor a coffee in the Verandah café with bread and butter.*"

**Adolphe Saafeld, first-class passenger**

### A DECK: COVERED FIRST-CLASS PROMENADE
*You are standing in the covered first-class promenade area. It stretched for 499 ft (152 m), more than the length of six tennis courts, so there was plenty of space to stroll.*

Teak deck chairs, known as steamer chairs, could be reserved before the voyage began or rented while the ship was at sea.

### A WALK ON DECK
The Promenade Deck, reserved for the use of first-class passengers, was a very lively place. Passengers would chat as they walked around or sat in deck chairs enjoying the sea air. It was sheltered from rain and bad weather by the Boat Deck above.

## LOUNGING AROUND

For snacking between meals, there were three first-class cafés: the Verandah, the Palm Court, and the Café Parisien. Families with children tended to choose the Verandah Café, while fashionable young people preferred the stylish Café Parisien.

The Café Parisien was like a fashionable Paris café, with the added advantage of a sea view through large picture windows.

The decorated china cups that first-class passengers sipped their tea from were specially made for *Titanic*.

## KEEPING FIT

The gymnasium was up on the Boat Deck and had the latest equipment, including rowing and cycling machines, plus an electric camel and two electric horses! A fitness instructor, like a personal trainer, was on hand to help passengers use the machines.

Thomas McCawley, *Titanic's* fitness instructor, demonstrates how to use the rowing machine.

A richly carved screen over the portholes cast patterns of light on the walls to create an exotic atmosphere.

## TURKISH BATH

The Turkish bath was decorated with colorful blue and green tiles and Arabian-style lamps. It had a steam room, hot and cool rooms, and even an electric bath—an early version of a sunbed where passengers could get a tan.

# A DIP IN THE POOL

On the middle deck of *Titanic*, next to the Turkish bath, there was a swimming pool for the first-class passengers. This was one of the first swimming pools to be installed on an ocean liner.

## DIVE IN

Visitors to the Turkish bath, hot from the sauna and steam room, would cool down with a refreshing plunge in the pool. Others went straight to the pool to swim laps, working up an appetite for their next big meal.

A White Star publicity painting of the pool shows bathers in blue knitted swimsuits.

Alongside the pool were a row of changing rooms and showers.

"*...met the professional racquet player in a half-hour's warming up for a swim in the six-foot (2-m) deep tank of saltwater heated to a refreshing temperature.*"

**Colonel Archibald Gracie, first-class passenger**

COLONEL ARCHIBALD GRACIE

## F Deck: The Swimming Pool

*You are standing by the swimming pool, which was 29 ft (9 m) long, 14 ft (4 m) wide, and 6 ft (2 m) deep. It was filled with sea water, warmed to room temperature by the ship's boilers. When the ship was moving, the pool's surface rippled with vibrations.*

# DINNER IS SERVED

For the first-class passengers, dinner on *Titanic* was a grand occasion. They dressed elegantly for dinner, with the men all wearing identical black tailcoats and white bow ties. The ladies wore expensive gowns and their finest jewelery.

This first-class menu shows the wide variety of dishes available for dinner.

### R.M.S. "TITANIC"

APRIL 10, 1912.

HORS D'ŒUVRE VARIÈS

CONSOMMÉ RÉJANE        CRÈME REINE MARGOT

TURBOT, SAUCE HOMARD
WHITEBAIT

MUTTON CUTLETS & GREEN PEAS
SUPRÊME OF CHICKEN À LA STANLEY

SIRLOIN OF BEEF, CHÂTEAU POTATOES
ROAST DUCKLING, APPLE SAUCE
FILLET OF VEAL & BRAISED HAM

CAULIFLOWER                    SPINACH
BOILED RICE
BOVIN & BOILED NEW POTATOES

PLOVER ON TOAST & CR
SALAD

PUDDING SANS
CHARLOTTE CO
GRANVIL

FRENCH ICE

*Titanic* carried 44,000 pieces of cutlery, 29,000 glasses, and 57,600 plates and bowls.

## DINNER TIME!
Before dinner, people gathered in the First-class Reception Room. They waited until the serving of dinner was announced by the ship's bugler, P.W. Fletcher, who played a tune called the "Roast Beef of Old England."

## THE FINEST FOOD
Dinner had up to eleven courses, each served with a different wine. The French-style dishes were as good as those served in the best restaurants. Passengers could enjoy everything from a first course of oysters to a dessert of French ice cream.

## TABLE MANNERS
Dinner could last several hours and followed strict rules. Different plates, glasses, and cutlery were used for each course, many decorated with the White Star emblem.

You are standing in the First-class Dining Saloon, which was 115 ft (35 m) long and could seat 532 diners. It was luxuriously decorated in the style of a stately English home from the early seventeenth century.

"*Fancy strawberries in April and in mid-ocean. The whole thing is positively uncanny.*"

**Lady Duff Gordon, first-class passenger**

LADY DUFF
GORDON

# SECOND CLASS

*Titanic's* 285 second-class passengers were delighted with their cabins. They were in fact as luxurious as first class on many other ships.

## A DIFFERENT CLASS

Second-class passengers were also impressed by the high-quality meals served in the Second-class Saloon, where a pianist played as they ate. In those days, men and women usually separated after dinner. The men went off to the smoking room, while women went to the library or lounge.

## COZY CABINS

The cabins were small, but comfortable, with up to four bunk beds, screened by curtains. There was a mahogany cabinet with a mirror, washbasin, and tap for cold water. Passengers could ask their stewards to bring jugs of hot water.

Second-class passengers stroll on their own section of the Boat Deck, with folded deck chairs to the right.

A White Star Line publicity picture shows a two-person second-class cabin, complete with a comfortable sofa to relax on.

## BOAT DECK: SECOND-CLASS PROMENADE

*You are standing in the second-class promenade area, which was in the rear part of the Boat Deck. The deck in front is divided into other promenade areas: for the engineers, first-class passengers, and officers.*

MINNEAPOLIS
MIA INSTITUTE
OF ARTS

Visiting the
MIA is easy!
www.artsmia.org

**FREE**
General admission
and parking are free
every day.

Free parking available
on Third Avenue in
the ramp and on two
surface lots.

**MUSEUM HOURS**
Sunday      11 A.M.–5 P.M.
Monday      Closed
Tuesday     10 A.M.–5 P.M.
Wednesday   10 A.M.–5 P.M.
Thursday    10 A.M.–9 P.M.
Friday      10 A.M.–5 P.M.
Saturday    10 A.M.–5 P.M.

Minneapolis Institute of Arts
2400 Third Avenue South
Minneapolis, MN 55404

**CONTACT US**
(612) 870-3131
www.artsmia.org

**Special thanks to the
Friends of the Institute**

Yoshimoto Nara, Japanese,
b.1959, Your Dog, 2002, fiberglass,
gift of Dr. George T. Shea and
Gordon Locksley

"*The s___ ___ a palace...my cabin has hot and cold water, a very comfy-looking bed, and plenty of room.*"

**Laurence Beesley, a teacher traveling
to the U.S. on vacation**

LAURENCE
BEESLEY

# In Steerage

Steerage was another name for third class. *Titanic* carried 706 third-class passengers. They came from more than 30 different countries, all hoping to find a new and better life in the U.S.

## A FUTURE IN AMERICA

The third-class passengers included 104 Swedes. They had already made a long journey across the North Sea to Hull and then by train to Southampton. Among them was Carl Asplund, a 40-year-old farm laborer, traveling with his wife and five children. He was sure that the U.S. would offer more opportunities than Sweden.

Carl Asplund carried this notebook, in which he had carefully copied an advertisement inviting settlers to move to California.

*"California wants people like you. Now is your time to come here."*

**Carl Asplund's notebook**

In Queenstown, Ireland, a U.S. doctor inspects the eyes of Irish steerage passengers for symptoms of trachoma.

## HEALTH CHECKS

Steerage passengers had to pass through strict health checks to be cleared for entry into the U.S. Before they could even board *Titanic*, they were checked for infectious diseases, such as trachoma, a disease causing blindness.

## THIRD-CLASS CABINS

Third-class cabins were on the lower decks, toward the bow and the stern, and closer to the noise of the engines. Although small, they were clean and modern, with electric light and heating and a washbasin filled with cold water from a cistern.

The third-class dining rooms had individual chairs instead of the benches found on most other ships.

A third-class cabin, with two bunk beds. These had blankets and pillows stuffed with feathers, but no sheets.

## ENTERTAINMENT

The ship had a Third-class General Room for families and a smoking room with a bar for the men. Every evening, the passengers gathered in the General Room to play music, sing, dance, and talk excitedly about their future in the U.S.

The General Room had white painted walls, decorated with colorful White Star Line posters of ships and their destinations.

## FOOD WITHOUT FRILLS

There were two third-class dining rooms, with white enamelled walls. There was room for 473 people, so the passengers ate in two sittings. Meals, such as corned beef with boiled potatoes, were simple but filling. Fruit and freshly baked bread were also served with every meal.

The crockery in third-class was simple, but everything was decorated with the White Star Line emblem.

# DISASTER STRIKES

On the evening of Sunday, April 14, *Titanic* was heading west, at slightly below top speed. There had been iceberg warnings, but Captain Smith didn't give the order to slow down.

### SOUNDING THE ALARM

At 11:40 pm, Frederick Fleet, a lookout in the crow's nest, saw a dark object in front of the ship. He rang his warning bell and telephoned the bridge, saying "Iceberg, right ahead!"

The bell in *Titanic*'s crow's nest was rung three times—the signal for danger right ahead.

### TURNING THE SHIP

On the bridge, First Officer William Murdoch told the helmsman, Robert Hitchens, to turn *Titanic* hard to port (left), and ordered the engineers to put the ship into reverse.

### THE ICEBERG STRIKES

*Titanic* slowly turned, but only enough to avoid a head-on collision. After an agonizing wait of 37 seconds, *Titanic* smashed into the iceberg along her starboard (right) side.

The ship's telegraph was used to tell the engineers below decks to change speed or reverse the ship.

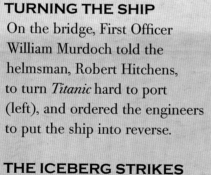

# ABANDON SHIP!

Shortly after the collision with the iceberg, Captain Smith and Thomas Andrews, *Titanic*'s builder, inspected the damage. Andrews told the captain that the ship was doomed and would sink in just two hours.

This iceberg, photographed in the Atlantic on April 12, may be the one that *Titanic* struck.

### ICE DAMAGE
The iceberg opened a 295 ft (90 m) gash along the ship's starboard side, flooding six of her watertight compartments. These were only watertight to a limited height. Once water reached the top of each compartment, it would spill over into the next one. Eventually, the ship would sink.

### LIFE JACKETS
Soon after midnight, Captain Smith gave orders to prepare to abandon ship. The crew, summoned by alarm bells, uncovered the lifeboats and handed out life jackets. There was a life jacket for everyone on the ship. A life jacket would keep its wearer afloat, but it gave no protection from the deadly cold of the icy sea.

*Titanic*'s life jackets were made from cork floats covered with canvas fabric.

# SLOWLY SINKING

As her forward compartments filled with water, *Titanic* slowly sank from the bow. On the bridge, Fourth Officer Boxhall fired distress rockets, hoping that they would be seen by another ship.

## LOADING THE LIFEBOATS

The crew helped people onto lifeboats, until the last two boats were launched by floating them straight off the sinking ship. After all the lifeboats had gone, more than 1,500 people remained on board *Titanic*.

## LEFT ON BOARD

Most of those who remained on the ship made their way to the rising stern, clinging to deck fittings and railings. As the deck grew too steep to stand on, some jumped into the icy sea, hoping to swim to a lifeboat. Even at this late stage, the ship's lights continued to shine, thanks to the engineers, who bravely remained at their posts.

## BOAT DECK: THE WHEELHOUSE

*You are standing in the wheelhouse of* Titanic, *where the helmsman steered the ship using the wheel. The room in front is the bridge, where the officer in charge of navigating the ship kept watch and gave orders.*

"*An iceberg, sir. I hard-a-starboarded and reversed the engines and I was going to hard-a-port around it, but she was too close.*" **First Officer William Murdoch**

FIRST OFFICER
WILLIAM MURDOCH

## NCH THE LIFEBOATS

ordered his officers to fill the lifeboats. Women
ildren were to be the first to board them. *Titanic*
lifeboats, enough to carry just 1,178 of the 2,223
on board. The only hope for passengers unable
a place in a lifeboat was that rescuers would
efore the ship sank.

On the Boat Deck, there were
14 large wooden lifeboats. Each
boat could hold 65 people.

This is the only photograph of a
radio operator at work on *Titanic*.
Radio messages could be received
up to 994 miles (1,600 km) away.

## SEND HELP!

At 12:10 am, Smith ordered the ship's
radio operators to send out distress
calls. Using Morse code, in which short
and long signals stand for letters, the
operators called for help. They
sent the traditional distress
signal, CQD, as well as
a recently introduced
new signal, SOS.

*"We are sinking fast. Passengers
are being put into boats."*

he last message sent by radio operator Jack Phillips

JACK
PHILLIPS

# TO THE LIFEBOATS

Panic and confusion grew as news of the emergency spread and the lifeboats were lowered. There had been no lifeboat drill, so many of the passengers and crew didn't know what to do.

## WOMEN AND CHILDREN FIRST

Officers Murdoch and Lightoller were in charge of the lifeboats on each side of the ship. They filled them with women and children first, plus a few crewmen to pull the oars. Many women did not want to leave their husbands behind and some lifeboats left the ship half-empty.

## THE LAST BOATS

As it became clear that the ship was really sinking, there was a scramble for places in the lifeboats. By the time the third-class passengers managed to find their way to the top deck, almost all of the lifeboats had gone.

The lifeboats had to be slowly lowered from a height of 59 ft (18 m) to the sea below.

This artist's impression shows the lifeboats being filled in an orderly way, with women saying goodbye to the men, who stand back.

*"There weren't enough boats to take half the people and the chances of the other half in that icy cold water were absolutely nil."*

**Second Officer Charles Lightoller**

CHARLES LIGHTOLLER

CHARLES HENDRICKSON

> "*It's up to us to go back and pick up anyone in the water.*"
>
> **Crewman Charles Hendrickson, on Lifeboat 1**

**CHARLES HENDRICKSON**

## THE LAST VIEW

Fearing being sucked under by the sinking ship, the lifeboat crews rowed as far away as possible. At 2:20 am, they watched as *Titanic* finally disappeared beneath the water. With the ship gone, the air was filled with cries for help from hundreds of people in the water.

Lifeboat 14, towing one of the canvas collapsible lifeboats, photographed on the morning after the sinking.

Moors Coutts Bank Ltd. April 16
Strand. London. W.C

Pay to J. Horswell, or order.
The Sum of. Five Pounds.

£ 5 . 0 . 0.
Cosmo Duff Gordon

Sir Cosmo Duff Gordon instructed his bank to pay each of the crewmen in his lifeboat.

## NO GOING BACK

In different lifeboats, Molly Brown, Charles Hendrickson, and Lady Rothes each suggested returning to pick up survivors. They were overruled by passengers who thought the boats would be swamped. One lady said, "Why should we all lose our lives in a useless attempt to save others from the ship?"

## LIFEBOAT FOR HIRE?

Lifeboat Number 1 could have gone back for more survivors. It was built to hold 40 people, but carried only twelve, including Sir Cosmo and Lady Duff Gordon. Sir Cosmo later gave money to the crewmen and was accused of hiring his own personal lifeboat.

**MOLLY BROWN**

**THE COUNTESS OF ROTHES**

## A Deck: Grand Central Staircase

*You are looking down at* Titanic's *Grand Central Staircase, as the waters rise, step by step. In a few moments, the lights will go out, and water from the deck above will smash through the glass dome over the staircase and into the ship.*

# LAST MOMENTS

Survivors later gave accounts of the bravery of those who went down with *Titanic*. Among those celebrated as heroes were the ship's musicians, who played as the ship sank, and the U.S. millionaire Benjamin Guggenheim.

### LIKE GENTLEMEN

Guggenheim made no effort to save himself and even refused to wear a life jacket. After helping to load the lifeboats, he returned to his cabin with his valet, where they put on full evening dress, to await their fate "like gentlemen."

To the end, *Titanic*'s musicians played lively tunes, to keep up the passengers' spirits.

BENJAMIN GUGGENHEIM

THE ILLUSTRATED LONDON NEWS, APRIL 27, 1912.—630

BRAVE AS THE "BIRKENHEAD" BAND: THE "TITANIC'S" MUSICIAN HEROES.

*"We've dressed up in our best and are prepared to go down like gentlemen."*

**Benjamin Guggenheim speaking to a steward**

# THE RESCUE

Although many ships received *Titanic's* radio distress calls, only one was close enough to help. This was the Cunard liner, RMS *Carpathia*, commanded by Captain Arthur Rostron.

## MESSAGE RECEIVED

When she received the distress call at 12:25 am, *Carpathia* was about 58 miles (93 km) southeast of *Titanic* and heading east. Captain Rostron immediately gave orders to change course. He prepared his ship in every detail, ordering hot drinks, soup, and medical supplies to be prepared, and cabins made ready for the survivors.

*Carpathia* was on her way from New York to Gibraltar when the distress call came from *Titanic.*

## MAXIMUM SPEED

*Carpathia* was supposed to have a maximum speed of 14 knots. However, by setting every stoker to work, Rostron boosted the ship's speed to over 17 knots. Unaccustomed to this power, the ship's decks shook as she steamed toward *Titanic.*

CAPTAIN ARTHUR ROSTRON

"*Icebergs loomed up and fell astern; we never slackened, though sometimes we altered course suddenly to avoid them.*"

**Captain Arthur Rostron, recalling the race to reach *Titanic***

PRESENTED
TO THE
CAPTAIN
OFFICERS & CREW
OF
R.M.S."CARPATHIA"
IN RECOGNITION OF GALLANT &
HEROIC SERVICES
FROM THE SURVIVORS
OF THE
S.S."TITANIC"
APRIL 15TH 1912

DIEGES & CLUST
N.Y.

The grateful survivors from *Titanic* later presented 320 medals to the crew of *Carpathia*.

## THE RESCUE BEGINS

*Carpathia* reached the scene of the disaster at 4 am, an hour and 45 minutes after *Titanic* had sunk. By now, the lifeboats were scattered over several square miles of sea. It took four hours for the rescuers to pick up all 706 survivors.

Huddled on the deck of *Carpathia*, the survivors are wrapped in blankets.

## SILENT SURVIVORS

Captain Rostron was struck by how quiet the survivors were. There was no celebration at being rescued. Many women had lost husbands and were suffering from shock and grief. Children who had lost their fathers still hoped that by some miracle they might be found.

## THE DEAD

The rescuers arrived too late for the passengers in the water, who all died in their first hour in the icy sea. Over the next few days, other ships would arrive to search for the dead. In all, 337 bodies were retrieved; 128 of them were buried at sea.

Survivors from Lifeboat 1, safely aboard *Carpathia*, including Sir Cosmo Duff Gordon (back row, third from left).

# AFTER THE TRAGEDY

News that *Titanic* had sunk quickly spread around the world. Everywhere, people were shocked and fascinated by the disaster. Within months, the first films, songs, and books about *Titanic* appeared.

## NEWS OF THE DISASTER

For weeks, news of the *Titanic* disaster and the loss of 1,517 lives filled the papers. Many stories were told of the heroic self-sacrifice of the crew and the male passengers who died. A myth also developed that *Titanic*'s builders had claimed she was "unsinkable."

## LESSONS LEARNED

In New York and London, there were inquiries into why the disaster had happened. Both concluded that *Titanic* was traveling too fast and recommended new safety regulations. Ships would now have to carry enough lifeboats for everybody on board.

A newspaper boy outside the White Star Line's office in London, on April 16, 1912.

TITANIC DISASTER GREAT LOSS OF LIFE
EVENING NEWS

J. Bruce Ismay, Managing Director of White Star Line, answers questions at the public inquiry into the disaster.

## REMEMBERING *TITANIC*

The loss of *Titanic* was felt most deeply in Southampton, home to 724 members of the crew, of whom only 175 survived. In 1914, more than 100,000 gathered here for the unveiling of a memorial to *Titanic*'s engineers.

The Southampton Memorial to the engineers on board *Titanic*, who died at their posts.

> "*Be British was the cry as the ship went down*
> *Every man was steady at his post*
> *Captain and crew when they knew the worst*
> *Saving the women and children first.*"
>
> Lyrics to "Be British" by Lawrence Wright, 1912

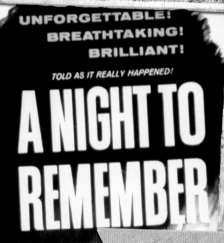

UNFORGETTABLE!
BREATHTAKING!
BRILLIANT!

TOLD AS IT REALLY HAPPENED!

# A NIGHT TO REMEMBER

A NEW MOTION PICTURE
Never before seen on
Screen or
Television!

The screenplay of *A Night to Remember* was based on interviews with survivors.

NOTHING ON EARTH
COULD COME BETWEEN THEM.

LEONARDO DiCAPRIO    KATE WINSLET

# TITANIC

*Titanic* used the disaster as the setting for a love story between passengers from different classes.

THE RANK ORGANIZATION presents
KENNETH MORE in
A NIGHT TO REMEMBER
Based on the book by WALTER LORD

## BE BRITISH!

Captain Smith, who died on *Titanic*, was declared a hero. According to one newspaper, Smith's last words, shouted through a megaphone, were "Be British!" This story inspired a popular song, released on record in 1912 to raise money for survivors.

## TITANIC MOVIES

There have been more than twenty movies about *Titanic*, the first two released within months of the sinking. The most historically accurate is *A Night to Remember* (1958). The best known is *Titanic* (1997), one of the most successful movies ever.

# TITANIC TODAY

*Titanic* still lies 12,464 ft (3,800 m) down, on the Atlantic seabed, where she sank a century ago. The wreck was discovered in 1985, by a joint French and U.S. expedition led by Dr. Robert Ballard.

## DISCOVERY

Ballard found the wreck after a two-month search using an unmanned mini-submarine. *Titanic* had split in two, with her bow and stern sections settling 1,968 ft (600 m) apart. Between them, debris from the ship lay scattered across the seabed.

The rusting bow of *Titanic* on the seabed, its railings still in place.

The bronze starboard propeller is perfectly preserved. Unlike iron, bronze does not rust.

China dishes stacked up in neat rows where they landed on the seabed.

## RELICS

Ballard believed that the wreck should be left untouched. However, in the 1990s, a U.S. company called RMS Titanic, Inc. began to salvage objects from the ship. Since then, more than 5,500 artifacts have been recovered and put on display in a series of traveling exhibitions.

## THE FUTURE OF *TITANIC*?

The wreck of *Titanic* is gradually collapsing, as the wrought iron of the ship is eaten away by metal-eating microbes. Nobody is quite sure how long the actual ship will survive, but our fascination with the most famous ship in history shows no signs of fading away. *Titanic* will never be forgotten.

This battered silk top hat belonged to one of the first-class passengers.